The
Sports Centre

Paul Humphrey
Photographs by Chris Fairclough

W
FRANKLIN WATTS
LONDON • SYDNEY

First published in 2006 by
Franklin Watts
338 Euston Road,
London NW1 3BH

Franklin Watts Australia
Hachette Children's Books
Level 17/207 Kent Street
Sydney NSW 2000

ISBN-10: 0 7496 6917 9
ISBN-13: 978 0 7946 6917 1

A CIP catalogue record for this book is available from the British Library.
Dewey Decimal Classification: 796.06

Planning and production by Discovery Books Limited
Editors: Rachel Tisdale and Paul Humphrey
Designer: Jemima Lumley
Photography: Chris Fairclough

The author, packager and publisher would like to thank the manager and
staff of the South Shropshire Leisure Centre, Ludlow, Shropshire, Ludlow
School, Ottilie and Auriel Austin-Baker, Lucas Tisdale and Jack Moran for
their help and participation in this book.

Printed in Malaysia

Contents

The sports and leisure centre

The sports and leisure centre is where people go to exercise, get fit and have fun.

They can lift weights
in the fitness suite.

This centre has two pools for swimming, diving and other water activities.

In the sports hall people come to play sports like football, judo, trampolining and karate. Badminton is another popular sport.

The team

More than 40 people work at the sports centre. Jon (below, left) is the centre **manager**, who looks after all of them.

Jon likes to keep his staff happy and here he shares a joke with Andrew, one of his duty officers.

Tom Williams (left) is a leisure assistant. Jon keeps in touch with him by **walkie-talkie**.

Shift work

The centre staff work in **shifts**. Some staff work in the mornings, some in the afternoons and some in the evenings. Here is the team from one shift.

Kletos is the health and fitness manager. He looks after the fitness suite.

'I enjoy working at the centre because I have lots of different jobs to do and no two days are the same.'
Tom, leisure assistant

Early start

The first shift starts at 6.30 in the morning. Sometimes it is still dark when Christian, one of the duty officers, arrives for work.

Jan, the assistant manager, arrives at the same time. She checks all the equipment in the store cupboard is in good condition. She makes sure the trampoline is safe to use.

Meanwhile, another duty officer, John, sets up the badminton nets, ready for the local school to use.

'The only things
I don't like about working at
the centre are the early starts.'
John, duty officer

Checking the pool

Jan checks the **chlorine** levels in the pool every morning. Chlorine helps kill any **germs** in the water.

The chlorine levels are a bit low, so Jan goes to the **basement** to adjust a **valve**. This lets more chlorine into the water. There are big machines in the basement that pump water around the pool and keep it warm.

The reception

The **reception** is the desk where people pay to go into the centre or make **bookings** for the different activities. Paula (right) is one of the **receptionists**. She is taking a booking on the phone.

'I get to meet lots of different people in my job.'
Paula, receptionist

Ami is a **customer** sales **advisor**. Her job is to help new members to join the centre or any of the clubs based there. She often works on reception, too.

Ottilie and Auriel have come in for a swim.
Receptionist Christiana tells them the cost
and takes their money.

Swimming Pool
Changing Area

This sign tells them
which way to go.

School visit

On weekdays the local schools use the centre for their sports and swimming lessons. A class from the local secondary school arrives in the sports hall.

Their teacher divides them into groups.

Some of the girls play netball.

The other
children
play
badminton.

The swimming pool

The swimming pool has **flumes**, a diving pool and a fun area as well as the main swimming pool.

Ottilie and Auriel like to play under the water fountain.

Charlotte, a leisure assistant, gets the small pool ready for a water **aerobics** class. The floor of the pool can be raised or lowered to change how deep it is. Now the floor is right at the top, so Charlotte can walk on it.

Here, the floor of the pool has been lowered, but the people doing the aerobics class can still touch the bottom.

Health and safety

Playing sports can be dangerous. All the staff at the sports centre have to be careful about safety.

'You have to stay very alert as a lifeguard. It feels like you have to be able to look in ten different places at once!'
Christian, duty officer

Most of the sports centre staff are trained **lifeguards**. At the pool, Christian sits in a high chair so that he can see what is going on. He blows his whistle if he sees anyone messing around.

Tom Waters is a leisure assistant and lifeguard. He talks to Auriel and Ottilie about pool safety.

The first aid room

Lucas has twisted his ankle. Duty officer Andrew and Lucas's friend Jack help Lucas to the first aid room.

In the first aid room Andrew binds Lucas's ankle with a bandage.

Staff meetings and training

Jon, the centre manager, meets with his staff once a week. Here, he is telling his staff how they can **recruit** more members.

The staff meeting is a chance for the staff to talk about any problems they have or to make suggestions.

At the staff meeting, they also plan the **schedules** for the different activities at the centre. Once the schedules are sorted out, Ami can type them into the computer.

Lifeguard training

Jon is responsible for training the lifeguards in rescue and life saving. They use a dummy to practise **resuscitation** techniques (right).

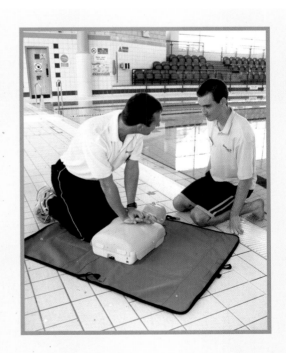

Now Mark and Martyn practise the chin-support tow (left).

Clubs and classes

Lots of different clubs and classes use the centre in the evenings and at weekends.

Martyn helps to run the swimming club. The children can get badges and **certificates** for their swimming.

The junior judo club meets every Monday. The children have to wear a special outfit called a *judogi*. The instructors show them what to do.

There is also a trampoline club.

The fitness suite

There are lots of different machines in the fitness suite. People can watch TV while they exercise.

Kletos, the health and fitness manager, has to make sure that all the machines are working properly. He makes a repair to one of the running machines.

Doctor's orders

Sometimes doctors send their patients to the centre to get fit. Paul has been told that he needs to get more exercise. Fitness instructor Chris is taking Paul's **blood pressure**. Then he will draw up an exercise **routine** for Paul.

When Paul returns the next day, Chris shows him how one of the machines works.

'I feel I can really make a difference when people come in unfit and I can help them to improve their health.'
Chris, fitness instructor

The dance studio

Kerrie is one of the fitness
class instructors in the
dance studio. Here,
she is dressed for a
'boxercise' class.

Kerrie tells the class what to do through
her microphone and **PA system**. The music in the
background helps the class to keep in rhythm.

These people are following Claire's instructions in their studio cycling class.

The crèche

If people using the dance studio have children they can leave them in the **crèche** while they exercise. Crèche assistant Debbie is looking after baby Jack.

The café

After visiting the fitness suite or swimming in the pool, customers can enjoy a meal or drink in the centre's café.

Catering manager Sue is cooking pasta with tomato sauce for a customer.

Catering assistant Lizzie fills up the counter with fresh snacks.

Auriel and Ottilie are enjoying a tasty sandwich and a fruit juice after their swim.

for the healthier choice...

for the healthier snack...

for the healthier you...

eme CAFÉ

at South Shropshire Leisure Centre
Bromfield Road • Ludlow • SY8 1DR
Phone direct: 01584 877077

Healthy eating

The café at the centre only serves healthy food, like pasta, fruit, salads and healthy snacks.

'There's no point in people doing lots of healthy exercise and then eating unhealthy food in the café afterwards!'

Jon, centre manager

the healthier choice

fresh pasta
fresh salads
wholemeal bread
speciality teas
pure fruit juice
free range eggs
quality de-caff coffee
organic milk shakes
local spring water
soup-of-the-day
homemade cookies
& flapjacks
freshly made
sandwiches
lo-salt
gluten free

The end of the day

The centre closes at 10 o'clock at night, but there are still things for the staff to do after all the customers have left.

Leisure assistant Ruth cleans around the pool with a mop.

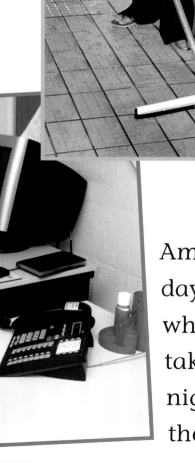

Ami counts the day's **takings**, which are then taken to the night safe at the bank.

It's 10.30 and nearly time to go home. Andrew locks all the doors.

Then he sets the alarm.

The centre is ready for another day.

Glossary

advisor someone who helps you to make choices.

aerobics exercises that make your heart beat faster and pump blood around your body more quickly.

basement the floor in a building below ground level.

blood pressure the strength of the flow of blood around your body.

bookings a particular time and place where you are going to do something.

certificates documents awarded to someone who has successfully completed something.

chlorine a chemical that kills germs.

crèche a place where very young children are looked after.

customer someone who goes into a place to buy something.

flumes long, tunnel slides at a swimming pool.

germs very tiny living things that can harm you.

lifeguard someone at a swimming pool or beach that looks after people in the water.

manager someone who is in charge of a place.

PA system a system of microphone, amplifier and loudspeakers that make someone's voice louder.

reception the area at the front of a building where you go to make enquiries.

receptionist someone who works on the reception.

recruit to persuade someone to join something.

resuscitation getting someone breathing again when their breathing has stopped.

routine doing the same thing over and over again.

schedules lists of things that are happening, with dates and times.

shifts the period of hours that people work.

takings the amount of money collected from customers.

valve a device that opens and closes to let more or less of something pass through it.

walkie-talkie a wireless telephone set.

Further Information

Books
Judo (Starting Sport series), Rebecca Hunter, Franklin Watts, 2006

Netball (Starting Sport series), Rebecca Hunter, Franklin Watts, 2006

Why Must I Take Exercise? (Why Must I series), Jackie Gaff, Evans Brothers, 2004

Your Body (Look After Yourself series), Claire Lewellyn, Franklin Watts, 2002

Websites
There are four sports councils in Britain. Their websites are:
www.sportengland.org
www.sportscotland.org.uk
www.sportni.org
www.sports-council-wales.co.uk
Australian Sports Commission: www.ausport.gov.au

Every effort has been made by the Packagers and Publishers to ensure that these websites contain no inappropriate or offensive material. However, because of the nature of the Internet, it is not possible to guarantee that the contents of these sites will not be altered. We strongly advise that Internet access is supervised by a responsible adult.

Index